REDESIGNED BY GRACE

A 50 Day Journey From Brokenness To Purpose

Stephanie E. Tudor

REDESIGNED BY GRACE

A 50 DAY JOURNEY FROM BROKENNESS TO PURPOSE

This Journal belongs to:

———————————————————————————

BY: STEPHANIE E. TUDOR

Copyright © 2025 Stephanie E. Tudor

All rights reserved. No part of this publication may be reproduced, distributed, or transmitted in any form or by any means, including photocopying, recording, or other electronic or mechanical methods, without the prior written permission of the publisher, except in the case of brief quotations embodied in critical reviews and certain other noncommercial uses permitted by copyright law. For permission requests, email the publisher:
Attention: Permissions Coordinator
Welcome To The Storm Publishing!
info@w2tspublishing.org

Ordering Information:
Quantity sales. Special discounts are available on quantity purchases by corporations, associations, and others. For details, contact the publisher at the email address above.
Orders by U.S. trade bookstores and wholesalers.
Library of Congress Control Number: 2025923793
ISBN: 9781966612919
Cover Design: Olaniyan Bukola
Formatter: The Storm Publishing
First Printed Edition: December 2025
Printed in the United States of America

DEDICATION

To every reader whose chapters feel torn.
May these pages remind you that God is not done with you.
Your story is being rewritten with grace and glory.
Whether you stayed or walked away, know this:
The Lord never left.
He is the One who saves, restores, and heals.
You are being ReDesigned By Grace.

How to Use This Devotional Workbook

Welcome, beloved. This 50-day journey is for us-the women who have felt forgotten, broken, silenced, or ashamed. Whether you're still in a difficult relationship or finding your way after one, this devotional is a safe space to heal, rediscover who you are in Christ, and remember that you are never beyond God's reach.

Each day offers:

- A Focus Scripture to guide your thoughts
- A devotional Reflection rooted in truth and compassion
- A Prayer to help you connect with God's presence
- A Journal Prompt for processing and personal growth
- Space to pour out your heart in writing You don't have to have it all figured out.

You just have to be willing to take the next step. God is already holding you. He is redesigning your life-by grace.

DAY 1

Broken but Not Beyond Repair

Scripture: Jeremiah 18 : 4 (KJV)

"And the vessel that he made of clay was marred in the hand of the potter: so, he made it again another vessel, as seemed good to the potter to make it."

Message

"Life has a way of breaking us in unseen places. But even when our hearts feel cracked, we are never beyond repair. The Potter sees value in our fragments. He does not discard the marred clay but remolds it with patience and purpose. Today, release the guilt of your past and trust that God's hands still know how to make you over again."

Prayer

"Father, thank You for seeing value in my broken pieces. When I feel unworthy, remind me that Your hands still hold me together. Teach me to trust Your shaping even when I don't understand it. In Jesus' name, Amen.

The Grace Move: Spend five minutes in silence, asking God to show you one area of your life He wants to restore.

DAY 2

Held by the Potter's Hands

Scripture: Jeremiah 18 : 6 (KJV)

"O house of Israel, cannot I do with you as this potter? saith the Lord. Behold, as the clay is in the potter's hand, so are ye in mine hand, O house of Israel."

Message

"God's hands are steady even when life spins out of control. The wheel is the process; His hands are the stability. You may not understand every turn, but each rotation has a purpose. Stay on the wheel—He is working something good through every season."

Prayer

"Lord, keep me steady when life feels unsteady. Help me to rest in the safety of Your hands. Remind me that every turn of the wheel is bringing me closer to the purpose You've designed for me. Amen."

The Grace Move: Write a short prayer thanking God for not letting go of you when you felt unworthy.

DAY 3

Grace in the Marred Places

> **2 Corinthians 12 : 9 (KJV)**

"And he said unto me, My grace is sufficient for thee: for my strength is made perfect in weakness. Most gladly therefore will I rather glory in my infirmities, that the power of Christ may rest upon me."

Message

"The enemy wants you to hide your flaws, but God uses them to reveal His glory. Your cracks become the very places where His light shines through. Don't curse the process; celebrate the grace that keeps you even when you are marred."

Prayer

"Heavenly Father, thank You that Your grace covers what's imperfect in me. Let Your light shine through every crack and remind me that weakness is where Your strength is made perfect. I receive Your grace today. Amen."

The Grace Move: List three areas where you see God's strength at work in your weakness.

_____
_____
_____
_____

DAY 4

The Wheel Keeps Turning

Jeremiah 18 : 3 (KJV)

"Then I went down to the potter's house, and, behold, he wrought a work on the wheels."

Message

"Life's wheel represents movement under God's control. Even when you feel stuck, He is still turning the wheel. Each rotation shapes character, faith, and purpose. Don't fight the turning—surrender to it."

Prayer

"Gracious God, thank You that the wheel never stops turning in Your divine rhythm. Even when I can't see progress, help me to trust that You are shaping my faith and building my endurance. Keep me pliable in Your hands. Amen."

The Grace Move: Journal about a season that felt painful but produced growth.

DAY 5

In the Potter's House

Jeremiah 18 : 2 (KJV)

"Arise, and go down to the potter's house, and there I will cause thee to hear my words."

Message

God invites you to a place of revelation—His house of healing and instruction. When you come to the Potter's house, He causes you to hear. Listening brings understanding, and understanding births transformation.

Prayer

Father, draw me daily into Your house of healing. Help me to listen with my heart and not just my ears. Let every word You speak reshape my life until I reflect Your image. In Jesus' name, Amen.

The Grace Move: Spend time in quiet worship today; listen for God's gentle whisper.

DAY 6

Shaped in the Fire

Isaiah 48 : 10 (KJV)

"Behold, I have refined thee, but not with silver; I have chosen thee in the furnace of affliction."

Message

"The fire is never meant to destroy you but to Transform you. In the furnace of affliction, God burns away impurities that would limit His reflection in your life. What feels unbearable is often preparation for visibility and strength."

Prayer

"Heavenly Father, refine me through the fires of testing without allowing the flame to consume me. Burn away everything that keeps me from reflecting Your image. Strengthen my faith and help me to trust Your refining work. Amen."

The Grace Move: Write about a fiery situation that produced greater faith in you.

_____
_____
_____
_____
_____

DAY 7

When the Pieces Don't Fit

Romans 8 : 28 (KJV)

"And we know that all things work together for good to them that love God, to them who are the called according to his purpose."

Message

"Sometimes you won't see how your pieces fit together until God arranges them. The shattered parts of your past are puzzle pieces of purpose. Trust His hands to align what you can't understand."

Prayer

"Lord, thank You for taking the scattered pieces of my life and arranging them with purpose. When I can't see the pattern, teach me to trust Your plan. Let my brokenness become beauty in Your timing. Amen."

The Grace Move: List three lessons you've learned from disappointment.

_____
_____
_____
_____
_____

DAY 8

The Process of Becoming

Philippians 1 : 6 (KJV)

"Being confident of this very thing, that he which hath begun a good work in you will perform it until the day of Jesus Christ."

Message

"Becoming is a process, not an event. The Potter is not finished with you yet. He is faithful to complete what He started. Don't rush the wheel; trust the timing of God's hands."

Prayer

"Gracious God, thank You for never giving up on the work You began in me. Help me to wait patiently while You shape and complete my purpose. I surrender to Your timing and Your touch. Amen."

The Grace Move: Write a short letter to yourself thanking God for the growth He has already produced in you.

DAY 9

Purpose in the Pain

Psalm 34 : 18 (KJV)

"The Lord is nigh unto them that are of a broken heart; and saveth such as be of a contrite spirit."

Message

"Pain pushes us toward purpose. Every tear has taught you something about God's nearness. Don't waste your pain—let it become proof that He dwells close to the brokenhearted."

Prayer

"Father, thank You for meeting me in my pain and turning sorrow into strength. Use every tear as testimony of Your presence. Teach me to see purpose even in what hurts most. Amen."

The Grace Move: Reflect on how your pain has drawn you closer to God.

DAY 10

Still on the Wheel

Jeremiah 18 : 3-4 (KJV)

"Then I went down to the potter's house, and, behold, he wrought a work on the wheels."

Message

"Even when you think you're finished, God places you back on the wheel for fine-tuning. He's not punishing you—He's perfecting you. Stay pliable in His hands; the end product will be worth the process."

Prayer

"Heavenly Father, when You return me to the wheel, help me to yield with gratitude instead of resistance. Smooth out what's rough and strengthen what's weak until my life reflects Your perfection. Amen."

The Grace Move: Journal a prayer of surrender to God's ongoing work in you.

DAY 11

When God Presses Pause

Ecclesiastes 3 : 1 (KJV)

"To every thing there is a season, and a time to every purpose under the heaven."

Message

"God's pauses are purposeful. When progress feels delayed, remember that the Potter never abandons His clay. He pauses to let the form settle so the next shaping won't collapse. Waiting seasons aren't wasted—they're strengthening you for what's next."

Prayer

"Lord, thank You for teaching me patience when life seems to stand still. Remind me that Your timing is perfect, even when I feel forgotten. Help me to rest in the pause and trust Your divine preparation. Amen."

The Grace Move: Write a prayer of gratitude for the seasons when God told you to wait.

DAY 12

The Power of Yielding

Romans 12 : 1 (KJV)

"I beseech you therefore, brethren, by the mercies of God, that ye present your bodies a living sacrifice, holy, acceptable unto God, which is your reasonable service."

Message

"Yielding isn't losing—it's aligning. When clay resists the potter's touch, it cracks. When it yields, it takes shape. God doesn't need your perfection; He desires your permission. Let Him shape you freely."

Prayer

"Heavenly Father, help me to surrender every part of me to Your will. Remove the resistance in my heart and teach me to yield completely to Your touch. Shape me into a vessel that pleases You. Amen."

The Grace Move: Journal about an area where you're learning to yield instead of control.

DAY 13

Lessons from the Wheel

> **Jeremiah 18 : 3 (KJV)**

"Then I went down to the potter's house, and, behold, he wrought a work on the wheels."

Message

"The wheel never stops spinning while the potter is working. Every turn teaches trust. The speed may vary, but the purpose remains—transformation. The same hand that spins the wheel also secures the vessel."

Prayer

"Gracious God, thank You for the lessons You teach me with every turn of the wheel. When life feels uncertain, remind me that Your hands are steady. Keep me centered in Your will and teach me through each rotation. Amen."

The Grace Move: List what you're learning in this current season of rotation and change.

_____

_____

_____

_____

_____

DAY 14

The Beauty of Brokenness

Psalm 51 : 17 (KJV)

"The sacrifices of God are a broken spirit: a broken and a contrite heart, O God, thou wilt not despise."

Message

"Brokenness invites beauty because humility invites healing. God draws close to contrite hearts. The very pieces you want to hide are the ones He uses to display His mercy."

Prayer

"Father, thank You for finding beauty in my brokenness. Use every crack to display Your mercy and love. Heal the areas that I've tried to hide and let Your grace make them whole. Amen."

The Grace Move: Write three ways God has brought beauty from your broken seasons.

DAY 15

Made Again

Jeremiah 18 : 4 (KJV)

"And the vessel that he made of clay was marred in the hand of the potter: so he made it again another vessel, as seemed good to the potter to make it."

Message

"Again" is God's favorite word for restoration. He never stops at ruined. When others give up, God starts over. You may not look like what you've been through, but grace has made you new again.

Prayer

"Heavenly Father, thank You for the power of 'again,' When I fall, lift me up and reshape me by Your grace. Let my life reflect the beauty of being made new in Your hands. Amen."

The Grace Move: Journal a declaration: "God is making me again."

DAY 16

Grace That Restores

> **1 Peter 5 : 10 (KJV)**

"But the God of all grace, who hath called us unto his eternal glory by Christ Jesus, after that ye have suffered a while, make you perfect, establish, strengthen, settle you."

Message

"Suffering doesn't mean you've been forsaken—it means you're being strengthened. Restoration is God's response to what the enemy thought would ruin you. After every breaking comes a building."

Prayer

"Lord, thank You for being the God who restores. When I feel weary, remind me that every trial is preparing me for strength. Restore what was lost and renew my heart with Your peace. Amen."

The Grace Move: Write a thank-You letter to God for the ways He has restored you after loss.

DAY 17

The Potter's Patience

> **Psalm 86 : 15 (KJV)**

"But thou, O Lord, art a God full of compassion, and gracious, long suffering, and plenteous in mercy and truth."

Message

"The Potter never rushes His work. He patiently refines, smooths, and reshapes until His reflection appears. Don't despise the slow pace—it's the rhythm of refinement."

Prayer

"Heavenly Father, thank You for Your patience with me. When I want to hurry ahead, slow my heart to match Your timing. Keep shaping me gently until Your image is clear in my life. Amen."

The Grace Move: List moments when God's patience has protected you from your own impatience.

DAY 18

When Purpose Hurts

Romans 8 : 18 (KJV)

"For I reckon that the sufferings of this present time are not worthy to be compared with the glory which shall be revealed in us."

Message

"Purpose is often wrapped in pain. The pressure you feel is proof that something divine is being developed inside you. Don't quit under the weight—what's forming in you is greater than what's against you."

Prayer

"Gracious God, thank You for trusting me with purpose even when it hurts. Help me endure the pressure with faith. Remind me that the pain I feel today is producing the glory You promised. Amen."

The Grace Move: Journal how God has turned your greatest pain into personal ministry.

DAY 19

Vessels of Honor

2 Timothy 2 : 21 (KJV)

"If a man therefore purge himself from these, he shall be a vessel unto honour, sanctified, and meet for the master's use, and prepared unto every good work."

Message

"God doesn't use perfect vessels—He uses prepared ones. Purity, humility, and obedience position you for purpose. Let Him cleanse the residue of the past so you can carry His glory without cracks of compromise."

Prayer

"Father, purify me so that I may be a vessel of honor fit for Your use. Cleanse me from everything that hinders Your presence. Fill me with Your Spirit and make me useful for Your kingdom. Amen."

The Grace Move: Write a short prayer dedicating yourself as a vessel of honor.

DAY 20

The Potter's Signature

> **Ephesians 2 : 10 (KJV)**

"For we are his workmanship, created in Christ Jesus unto good works, which God hath before ordained that we should walk in them."

Message

"Every masterpiece bears the artist's signature. God has marked you with His identity. You're not defined by what broke you but by Who rebuilt you. When others see you, they should see His handiwork."

Prayer

"Lord, thank You for placing Your signature on my life. Let everything I do bring glory to Your name. Help me to walk boldly as Your masterpiece, created for good works. Amen."

The Grace Move: Reflect on the unique ways God's fingerprints show up in your life story.

DAY 21

Lessons in the Waiting

Psalm 27 : 14 (KJV)

"Wait on the Lord: be of good courage, and he shall strengthen thine heart: wait, I say, on the Lord."

Message

"Waiting is where trust matures. The Potter often lets the clay rest between stages so it will hold its shape later. Don't rush the wait—God is preparing stability for what He's about to build through you."

Prayer

"Gracious God, teach me to wait with faith instead of frustration. Remind me that every pause has purpose. Strengthen my heart while I wait so that I can stand firm when You move. Amen."

The Grace Move: Journal one lesson you've learned while waiting on God's timing.

_____

_____

_____

_____

DAY 22

Faith Under Pressure

James 1 : 3–4 (KJV)

"Knowing this, that the trying of your faith worketh patience. ⁴But let patience have her perfect work, that ye may be perfect and entire, wanting nothing."

Message

"Pressure is proof of potential. When God allows the heat to rise, He is strengthening your faith for greater capacity. Every trial has purpose—endure it with expectation, not fear."

Prayer

"Father, when life presses hard against me, help me to see growth instead of defeat. Give me endurance that outlasts the trial and peace that outshines the pressure. I trust You through the process. Amen."

The Grace Move: Write about a time your faith grew stronger through testing.

_____
_____
_____
_____

DAY 23

Pieces of Purpose

> **Isaiah 61 : 3 (KJV)**

"To appoint unto them that mourn in Zion, to give unto them beauty for ashes, the oil of joy for mourning, the garment of praise for the spirit of heaviness; that they might be called trees of righteousness, the planting of the Lord, that he might be glorified."

Message

"God never wastes what was broken. Every fragment holds a future purpose. He collects your ashes and exchanges them for beauty. The pieces you thought were useless are ingredients for His glory."

Prayer

"Lord, thank You for taking the ashes of my past and turning them into something beautiful. Show me how every piece of my story can bring You glory. Help me to see purpose in what once felt lost. Amen."

The Grace Move: List three "ashes" God has turned into beauty in your life.

_____
_____
_____
_____
_____

DAY 24

The Power of Perspective

Philippians 4 : 11 (KJV)

"Not that I speak in respect of want: for I have learned, in whatsoever state I am, therewith to be content."

Message

"Perspective shifts pain into purpose. Paul learned contentment not in comfort but in Christ. When you change how you see a situation, you change how it shapes you. Stay grateful on the wheel."

Prayer

"Heavenly Father, open my eyes to see life from Your viewpoint. When circumstances overwhelm me, remind me that gratitude changes everything. Help me to stay content in You. Amen."

The Grace Move: Write a gratitude list for where you are right now.

DAY 25

The Potter's Plan

Jeremiah 29 : 11 (KJV)

"For I know the thoughts that I think toward you, saith the Lord, thoughts of peace, and not of evil, to give you an expected end."

Message

"Even when life feels uncertain, God's plan is unchanging. The Potter's intentions for you are peaceful and good. Trust that He sees the whole design when you only see a fragment."

Prayer

"Gracious God, thank You that Your plans for me are filled with peace and purpose. When I can't see the bigger picture, remind me that Your design is perfect. I choose to trust Your plan. Amen."

The Grace Move: Journal what it means to you that God's plans include you.

DAY 26

The Potter's Promise

> **Philippians 1 : 6 (KJV)**

"Being confident of this very thing, that he which hath begun a good work in you will perform it until the day of Jesus Christ."

Message

"God never starts what He won't finish. Every molding moment is a reminder of His commitment to complete you. Even when you feel unfinished, His hands are still faithful."

Prayer

"Heavenly Father, thank You for never leaving Your work undone. When I grow weary, remind me that You finish what You begin. Keep shaping me until I become the masterpiece You envisioned. Amen."

The Grace Move: Write a declaration: "God will finish what He started in me."

_____
_____
_____
_____
_____

DAY 27

Mended with Mercy

Lamentations 3 : 22–23 (KJV)

"It is of the Lord's mercies that we are not consumed, because his compassions fail not. ^{23} They are new every morning: great is thy faithfulness."

Message

Mercy is God's glue for broken people. Each morning brings fresh compassion to hold you together. You may have cracks, but you are not consumed—His mercy keeps you whole.

Prayer

Gracious God, thank You for new mercies every morning. When I feel like falling apart, hold me together with Your compassion. Let Your faithfulness be the strength that mends me daily. Amen.

The Grace Move: List three ways God's mercy has met you this week.

_____

_____

_____

_____

DAY 28

From Ruins to Renewal

Isaiah 61 : 4 (KJV)

"And they shall build the old wastes, they shall raise up the former desolations, and they shall repair the waste cities, the desolations of many generations."

Message

"God not only restores you—He uses you to rebuild others. Your testimony becomes a blueprint for renewal. What was once ruins in your life will now be a roadmap for someone else's redemption."

Prayer

"Father, thank You for turning my ruins into restoration. Use my story to rebuild hope in others. Let the lessons from my pain become the light that guides someone else to You. Amen."

The Grace Move: Write about a time God used your story to encourage another person.

_____

_____

_____

_____

DAY 29

Anointed for Purpose

2 Corinthians 1 : 21–22 (KJV)

"Now he which stablisheth us with you in Christ, and hath anointed us, is God; ²² Who hath also sealed us, and given the earnest of the Spirit in our hearts."

Message

"Anointing confirms assignment. You are sealed for service, not self-promotion. The oil flows over surrendered clay. Let God's anointing distinguish you—not for status, but for service."

Prayer

"Lord, thank You for anointing me with purpose. Keep my heart humble and my motives pure. Let Your Spirit empower me to serve with love and bring glory to Your name. Amen."

The Grace Move: Journal how you sense God calling you to use your gifts for His glory.

DAY 30

ReDesigned by Grace

Ephesians 2 : 8–10 (KJV)

"For by grace are ye saved through faith; and that not of yourselves: it is the gift of God:
⁹ Not of works, lest any man should boast.
¹⁰ For we are his workmanship, created in Christ Jesus unto good works, which God hath before ordained that we should walk in them."

Message

This is your transformation testimony—you are ReDesigned by Grace. God's workmanship is evident in every healed place, every restored dream, every renewed purpose. You are proof that grace still works.

Prayer

Heavenly Father, thank You for rewriting my story with grace. I am who I am because of Your mercy. Let my life forever declare that I have been redesigned by Your loving hands. Amen.

The Grace Move: Write your own short praise statement beginning with these words: "I am ReDesigned by Grace because ..."

DAY 31

In the Potter's Hands

Jeremiah 18:6

"O house of Israel, cannot I do with you as this potter? saith the Lord. Behold, as the clay is in the potter's hand, so are ye in mine hand, O house of Israel."

Message

"You are not forgotten on the wheel. The spinning, the pressure—it's all part of the Potter's process. God is not discarding you; He's redesigning you. What feels like breaking is actually reshaping. In His hands, you are safe. In His plan, you are becoming."

Prayer

"Lord, help me to trust You in the turning. Remind me that I am being held, not tossed aside."

The Grace Move: What part of your life feels like it's spinning right now? How can you surrender that area to the Potter?

DAY 32

Cracked But Not Crushed

> **2 Corinthians 4:8-9**

"We are troubled on every side, yet not distressed; we are perplexed, but not in despair;
⁹Persecuted, but not forsaken; cast down, but not destroyed."

Message

"Abuse can leave cracks that feel permanent. But God says you're not crushed. You are still here. And because of that, restoration is possible. The Potter knows how to fill the cracks with gold—making you even more precious."

Prayer

"God, I feel broken in places I can't even name. But I believe You are able to restore what's been damaged."

The Grace Move: Where have you felt crushed—and how has God kept you from being destroyed?

_____
_____
_____
_____
_____

DAY 33

The Whisper in the Silence

> **1 Kings 19:12**

"And after the earthquake a fire; but the Lord was not in the fire: and after the fire a still small voice."

Message

"Sometimes God doesn't shout. In the aftermath of chaos, He whispers. In the silence of suffering, He speaks gently. You don't have to hear Him through noise—listen in the stillness. He is near."

Prayer

"Lord, open my heart to hear Your whisper. In the quiet, speak peace to my storm."

The Grace Move: When was the last time you heard God's whisper? What did He say?

DAY 34

When You Feel Unseen

Genesis 16:13

"And she called the name of the Lord that spake unto her, Thou God seest me: for she said, Have I also here looked after him that seeth me?"

Message

"You may feel invisible in your pain—but not to God. He saw Hagar in the wilderness, and He sees you now. He sees your tears, your courage, and your heart. You are not alone. You are fully seen and deeply loved."

Prayer

"Father, thank You for seeing me when others overlook me. I rest in the comfort of Your eyes."

The Grace Move: What does it mean to you to be seen by God?

DAY 35

Peace in the Process

> **Isaiah 26:3**

"Thou wilt keep him in perfect peace, whose mind is stayed on thee: because he trusteth in thee."

Message

"Healing is a process, not a moment. Some days feel strong; others feel like setbacks. But peace isn't found in having it all together—it's found in keeping your mind on the One who holds you together."

Prayer

"Lord, teach me to fix my eyes on You, not the chaos around me. Give me peace in the process."

The Grace Move: What is one truth you can cling to today to anchor your peace?

_____
_____
_____
_____
_____

DAY 36

He Will Restore You

1 Peter 5:10

"But the God of all grace, who hath called us unto his eternal glory by Christ Jesus, after that ye have suffered a while, make you perfect, stablish, strengthen, settle you."

Message

"God promises restoration. Not just survival—but full, radiant, divine restoration. He will restore your joy, your identity, your voice. It may not be instant, but it is certain. He is faithful."

Prayer

"God, I hold onto Your promise of restoration. Restore me in every place that's been emptied."

The Grace Move: What does restoration look like to you? Where do you want God to restore you?

DAY 37

Beauty for Ashes

Isaiah 61:3

"To appoint unto them that mourn in Zion, to give unto them beauty for ashes, the oil of joy for mourning, the garment of praise for the spirit of heaviness; that they might be called trees of righteousness, the planting of the Lord, that he might be glorified."

Message

"Ashes come from what's been destroyed. But God trades ashes for beauty. You're not too burned, too far gone, or too damaged. His specialty is taking what's been ruined and making it radiant."

Prayer

"Jesus, I give You my ashes. Make something beautiful out of the parts I thought were too far gone."

The Grace Move: Where have you seen God begin to turn ashes into beauty in your life?

DAY 38

Chosen, Not Forgotten

John 15:16

"Ye have not chosen me, but I have chosen you, and ordained you, that ye should go and bring forth fruit, and that your fruit should remain: that whatsoever ye shall ask of the Father in my name, he may give it you."

Message

"You were not overlooked. You were chosen—by name, by love, by destiny. Abuse tells you you're unwanted. But God says, "I picked you." That truth silences every lie."

Prayer

"Lord, thank You for choosing me. Help me to believe I am worthy of that love."

The Grace Move: How does it feel to know you were chosen—not by accident, but on purpose?

DAY 39

Healing in His Wings

Malachi 4:2

"But unto you that fear my name shall the Sun of righteousness arise with healing in his wings; and ye shall go forth, and grow up as calves of the stall."

Message

"Healing is coming. Not just for your body—but for your soul, your memories, your future. Like the sun rises gently, God is rising over your life with healing. Let His warmth reach the cold places."

Prayer

"Lord, rise over my pain with healing in Your wings. Shine on the places I've hidden and feared."

The Grace Move: What area of your heart needs healing right now?

_____
_____
_____
_____
_____

DAY 40

Safe in His Arms

Psalm 91:4

"He shall cover thee with his feathers, and under his wings shalt thou trust: his truth shall be thy shield and buckler."

Message

"Safety is more than physical—it's emotional, spiritual, sacred. In God's presence, you are safe. Not judged. Not silenced. Held. Covered. Comforted. Rest in His embrace."

Prayer

"Father, let me find refuge in You. Wrap me in Your love and remind me I am safe with You."

The Grace Move: When do you feel safest in God's presence?

DAY 41

The Light in the Dark

Psalm 18:28

"For thou wilt light my candle: the Lord my God will enlighten my darkness."

Message

"Even the darkest season cannot snuff out the light God placed in you. He meets you there and kindles hope. When all seems dim, His flame still burns. You don't have to light the whole way—just take one step in faith. He'll do the rest."

Prayer

"Lord, You are my light when all feels lost. Brighten the path ahead and remind me that darkness is not the end."

The Grace Move: What dark place in your life is God shining His light into today?

_____
_____
_____
_____
_____

DAY 42

No Longer Bound

Galatians 5:1

"Stand fast therefore in the liberty wherewith Christ hath made us free, and be not entangled again with the yoke of bondage."

Message

"Abuse binds in ways we can't always see. But Jesus came to break every chain—mental, emotional, spiritual. Your past does not define your future. You are free to hope, to dream, to live. Not because of your strength, but because of His power."

Prayer

"Jesus, I receive the freedom You died to give me. Break off the old lies and help me walk in the truth of who I am in You."

The Grace Move: What do you want to be free from today—and what does freedom look like to you?

DAY 43

Nothing Wasted

Romans 8:28

"And we know that all things work together for good to them that love God, to them who are the called according to his purpose."

Message

"God wastes nothing. Not the pain. Not the tears. Not even the silence. He is able to repurpose it all for your good and His glory. It doesn't mean it was okay—but it does mean it can be redeemed."

Prayer

"God, I offer You every broken piece. Redeem what I've lived through and use it to birth something beautiful."

The Grace Move: *Where do you see God bringing purpose to your pain?*

DAY 44

He Calls You by Name

Isaiah 43:1

"But now thus saith the Lord that created thee, O Jacob, and he that formed thee, O Israel, Fear not: for I have redeemed thee, I have called thee by thy name; thou art mine."

Message

"You were never just "her" or "the one who went through it." You are known—deeply, intimately, lovingly. God doesn't define you by what happened. He defines you by His love. You are named. You are claimed. You are His."

Prayer

"Father, thank You for calling me by name. Help me see myself the way You see me."

The Grace Move: How does it feel to know God calls you by name and not by your past?

_____
_____
_____
_____
_____

DAY 45

Fully Seen, Fully Loved

> **Psalm 139:1-2**

"O lord, thou hast searched me, and known me.
² Thou knowest my downsitting and mine uprising, thou understandest my thought afar off."

Message

"So much of abuse causes us to hide—our thoughts, feelings, identity. But God sees it all and still loves you fully. He doesn't turn away from your truth. He embraces you right in the middle of it."

Prayer

"God, thank You for loving every part of me—even the parts I try to hide. Teach me to live unhidden before You."

The Grace Move: What parts of your story or self-do you need to bring into God's light today?

_____

_____

_____

_____

_____

DAY 46

Replanted and Restored

Isaiah 61:3

"To appoint unto them that mourn in Zion, to give unto them beauty for ashes, the oil of joy for mourning, the garment of praise for the spirit of heaviness; that they might be called trees of righteousness, the planting of the Lord, that he might be glorified."

Message

"What was uprooted will be planted again. You will not remain in the soil of sorrow. God replants with intention—strong, stable, rooted in Him. Your life will bear fruit again. Restoration isn't a return to what was; it's a birth of what's new."

Prayer

"God, plant me again. In joy. In peace. In hope. Let my life grow strong in You."

The Grace Move: Where do you sense God asking you to take root again?

DAY 47

A Voice Restored

> **Psalm 40:3**

"And he hath put a new song in my mouth, even praise unto our God: many shall see it, and fear, and shall trust in the Lord."

Message

"Abuse silences us. But God gives us our voices back. Your voice matters. Your story carries power. What once was suppressed will now rise in song. Not shame—but testimony."

Prayer

"Lord, restore my voice. Give me courage to speak again—over myself and into others."

The Grace Move: What would you say today if fear weren't in the way?

_____
_____
_____
_____

DAY 48

Grace Enough

2 Corinthians 12:9

"And he said unto me, My grace is sufficient for thee: for my strength is made perfect in weakness. Most gladly therefore will I rather glory in my infirmities, that the power of Christ may rest upon me."

Message

"You don't have to be enough—because His grace already is. When strength runs out, grace rises up. It carries. It comforts. It covers. Lean on Him."

Prayer

"Jesus, be my strength. Let Your grace flood the places where I feel empty or exhausted."

The Grace Move: Where do you need to lean on God's grace today?

_____
_____
_____
_____
_____

DAY 49

Rewritten by Love

Revelation 21:5

"And he that sat upon the throne said, Behold, I make all things new. And he said unto me, Write: for these words are true and faithful."

Message

"Your story isn't over. The chapter of pain is not the final word. God is the Author, and He is writing a redemptive ending. You are being rewritten—not by shame, but by love."

Prayer

"Lord, thank You for rewriting my story. I trust You with the pen."

The Grace Move: If you could rewrite one chapter of your story with God, what would it be?

_____
_____
_____
_____
_____

DAY 50

Redesigned by Grace

Ephesians 2:10

"For we are his workmanship, created in Christ Jesus unto good works, which God hath before ordained that we should walk in them."

Message

"You are not a mistake. Not a mess. Not a leftover. You are a masterpiece in progress—redesigned by grace. Your life is a work of divine art, shaped by mercy, finished in glory. Walk in that truth. Live like you belong to the Potter."

Prayer

"God, I receive the truth that I am Your workmanship. Let my life reflect Your love and grace."

The Grace Move: What does it mean to you to be redesigned by grace?

About the Author

Stephanie 'Elaine' Tudor is a Licensed Practical Nurse, Licensed Minister, and holds a Bachelor's degree in Leadership & Ministry. She is a devoted wife, proud mother of three, and grandmother of six.
As the founder and owner of Rays of Sonshine Licensed Childcare & Learning Academy and Lady T's Wedding & Event Venue, Stephanie's passion for people shines through her commitment to serve families and her community with excellence, compassion, and grace.

As the visionary behind the #ReDesignedByGrace movement, Stephanie shares her own journey from brokenness to wholeness—testifying of God's power to restore what life tried to destroy. Her calling is to minister hope to women from all walks of life, reminding them that they are never too broken for God to use and never too far for Him to reach.

Through her devotional writing, ministry, and daily walk of faith, Stephanie encourages women to surrender to the Potter's process and embrace the beauty of being redesigned by grace

www.ingramcontent.com/pod-product-compliance
Lightning Source LLC
Chambersburg PA
CBHW050731010526
44107CB00009B/812